Abraham's Stars

Holding On To God's Promises

Acknowledgements

Unending thanks to my friends and family for their support in testing times

Special thanks to Joy, Ian and Walter for their time and consideration

Quotations taken from the New International Version of the Bible, published by Hodder and Stoughton, 1998

Winter child – Isaiah 9 v 6 and Luke 1 v 28 and vs 30-38
Sing praises to me – Psalm 148 vs 1-6
Always with you – Psalm 139 vs 13 – 16
Deep calls unto deep - Psalm 42 v 7 (title phrase)
Remember me – Isaiah 55 v 8 (paraphrase)

Rest – Isaiah 26 v 3 paraphrased from King James Bible
A love that brings you peace – refers to Genesis 15 v 5 & 22 v 17
I love you – To God be the glory - lyrics Fanny Crosby (1820 –1915)

Published by Behold Books bbooks345@gmail.com
www.beverleyhealy.artweb.com

Preface

A personal journey geographically from England to Ireland, coincided with a personal journey of faith. Learning to trust God in new and deeper ways led me to use my artistic talents differently. Originally very much an observer, these new paintings came from the heart, soaked in a foundation of prayer or praise.

This book brings together a collection of these paintings alongside reflections and verses that either inspired them or were articulated after they were made. The first lines, or "titles" from each page combine to create a poem, which has become the introduction to the book.

Inspiration comes from Biblical characters, such as Abraham, who walked the journey of faith in their time. Characters who sometimes seem so large or fantastical but were human like us, finding their way. For those who may be unfamiliar with Abraham's story, it can be found in Genesis and comprises many years standing on a promise that he would be the father of many nations. " 'Look now toward heaven, and count the stars if you are able to number them.' And He said to him, ' So shall your descendants be.' " (Genesis 15 v 5). The promises persisted, whilst in earthly reality he and his wife Sarah were old and getting older, still waiting for their first child together. His path was not smooth and he made some mistakes, but he is commended in Hebrews for his great faithfulness. This book is not particularly about Abraham but it is about faith and holding on to God's promises.

In short, this is an illustrated journey through the fields of hope and promise.

Beverley Healy

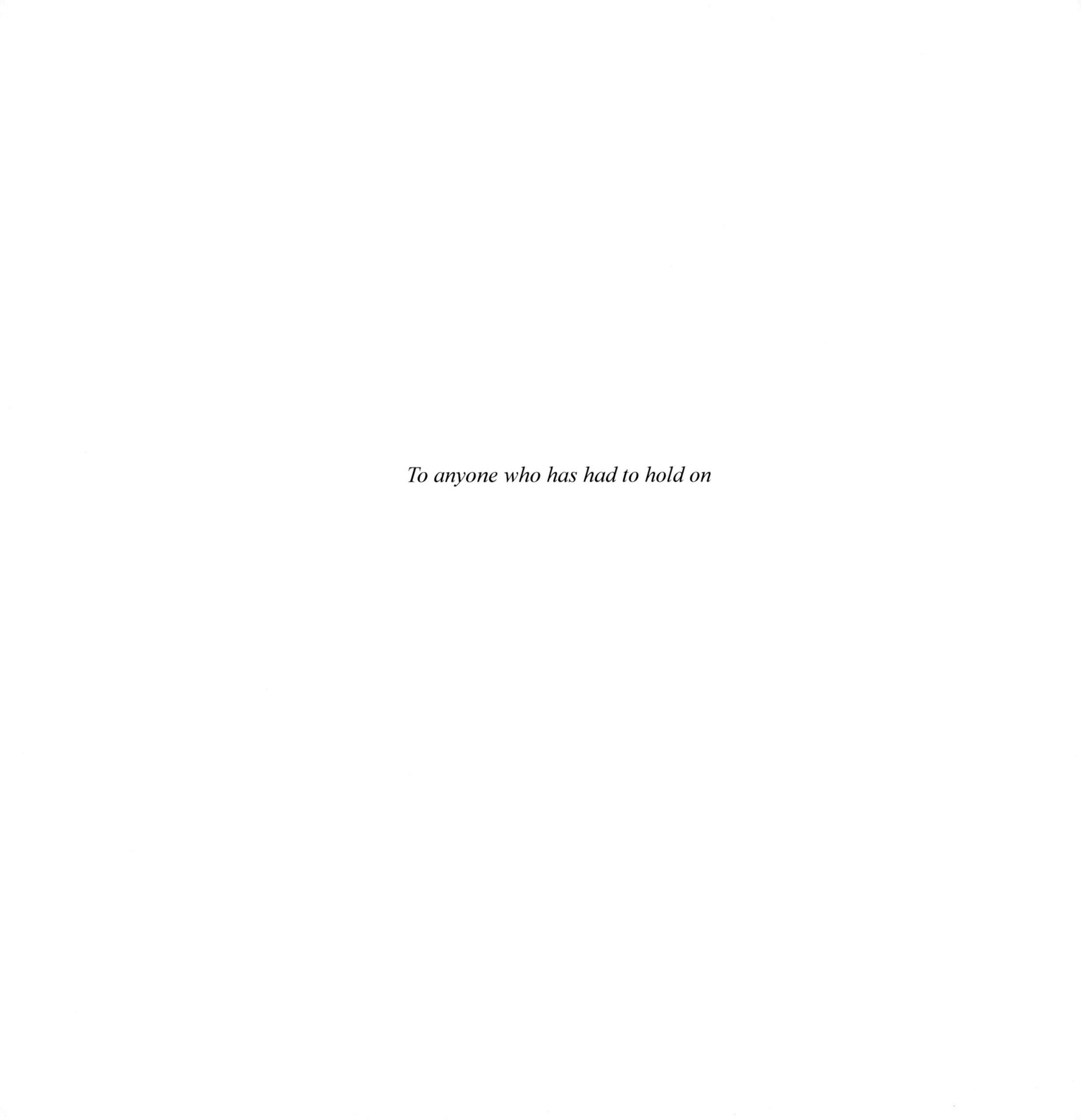

To anyone who has had to hold on

Abraham's Stars

Holding On To God's Promises

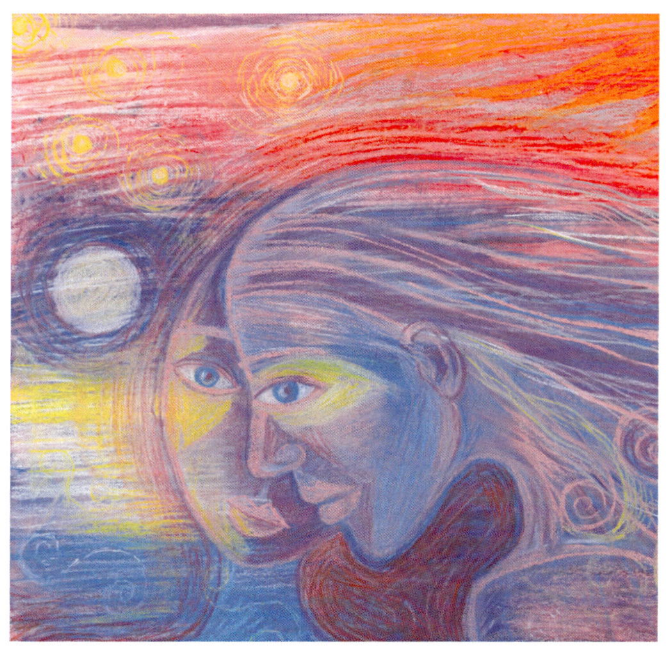

Winter child – I am with you
Sing praise to me; I am with you, I am yours
Always with you, always for you

A love that knows you, a love that knows your heart
A love that keeps its promises.
A love that hears your groaning,
A love that gives you peace.

Trust me

I will lift you up,
Deep will call unto deep,
Don't lose sight.
Praise me in the darkness,
Praise me through the pain.
Remember my promises,
Remember me.

A time will come

You will hold gold in your hands
And you will give it away.
There is hope and there is promise;
I love you.

Winter child – I am with you

A promise from long ago…..

"For unto us a child is born
Unto us a son is given
and the government will be upon his shoulders.
And he will be called
Wonderful Counsellor, Mighty God,
Everlasting Father, Prince of Peace."

"Greetings, you who are highly favoured!
The Lord is with you.
Do not be afraid Mary,
you have found favour with God.
You will be with child and give birth to a son
and you are to call his name Jesus.
He will be great and will be called
The Son of the Most High.
His kingdom will never end."

To you will be born a king, and you but a child yourself; 15,16 maybe? How did you feel? Imagine the honour, imagine the talk; apparent shame, but the honour, the privilege – this child born to be king.

Did you feel a winter chill – the thrill of it all, but the weight of it all. Winter child. Did you sit in silence for a while and touch your stomach with amazement – or even some trepidation? How amazing – this child born to you.

"And he will be called
Wonderful Counsellor, Mighty God
Everlasting Father, Prince of Peace."

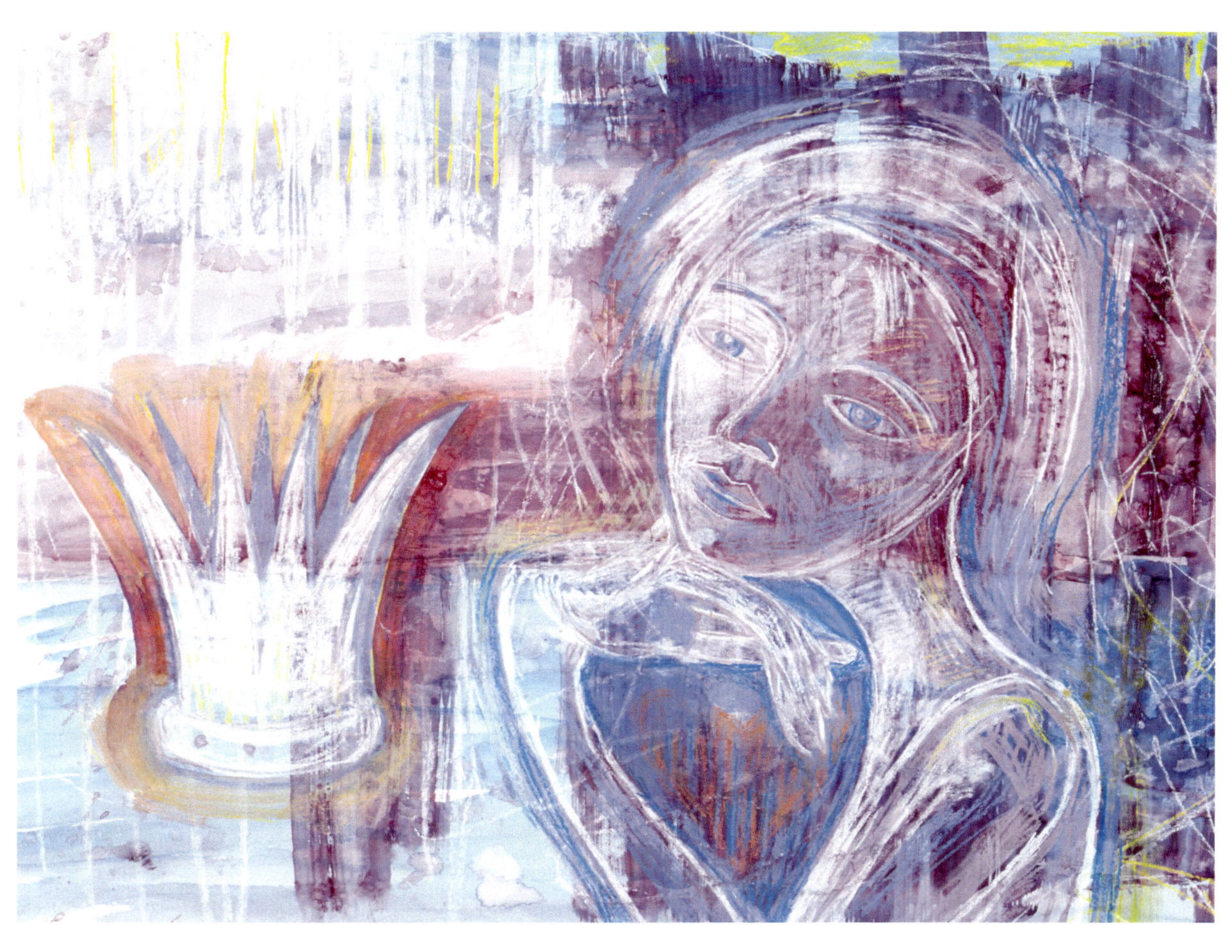

Sing praises to me. I am with you, I am yours

"Praise the Lord from the heavens,
praise him in the heights above.
Praise him, all his angels,
praise him, all his heavenly hosts.
Praise him sun and moon,
praise him all you shining stars.
Praise him, you highest heavens
and you waters above the skies.
Let them praise the name of the LORD
for he commanded and they were created.
He set them in place for ever and ever.
He gave a decree that will never pass away."

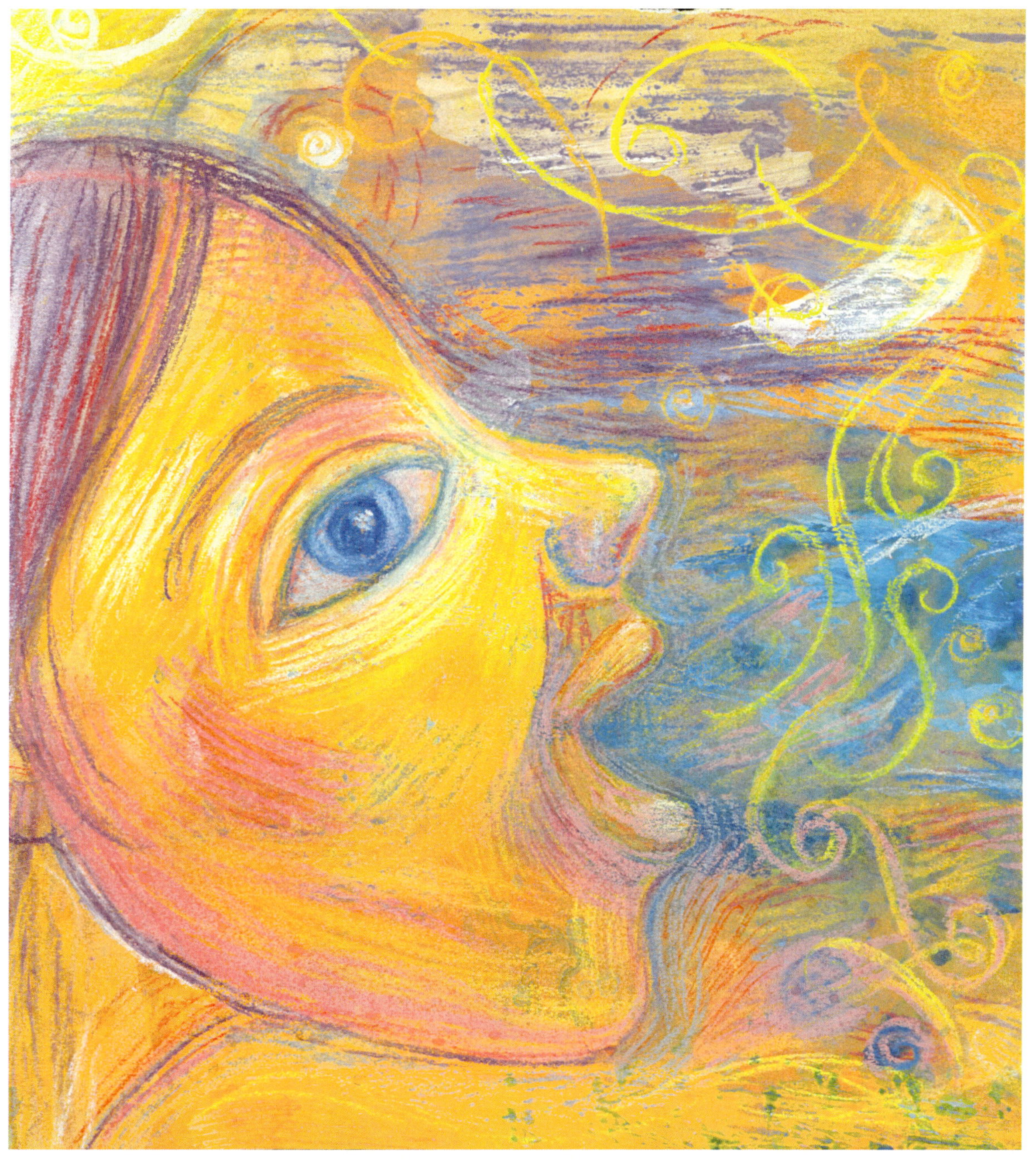

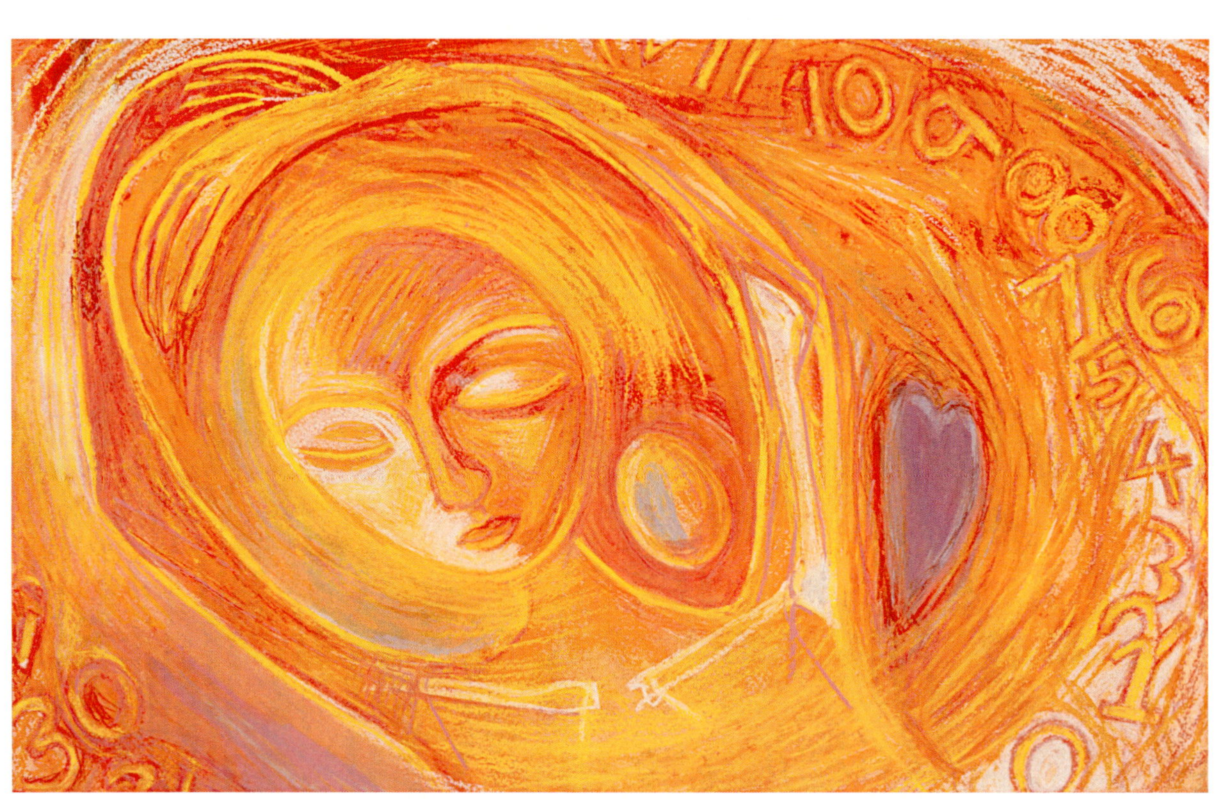

Always with you, always for you

"For you created my inmost being;
You knit me together in my mother's womb.
I praise you because I am fearfully
and wonderfully made;
Your works are wonderful,
I know that full well.
My frame was not hidden from you
when I was made in the secret place.
When I was woven together
in the depths of the earth
your eyes saw my unformed body.
All the days ordained for me
were written in your book
before one of them came to be."

A love that knows you, a love that knows your heart

Bearing a kiss on my cheek from your lips is what I wait for, long for and hope to come. Was it written in the stars? I can't be sure, but that you set the stars in place, that you allow them to shoot and fall, that you fulfil the desires of our hearts, that I know. So, bearing your kiss on my cheek I thank you for your unending love for me.

Your love for me never ends

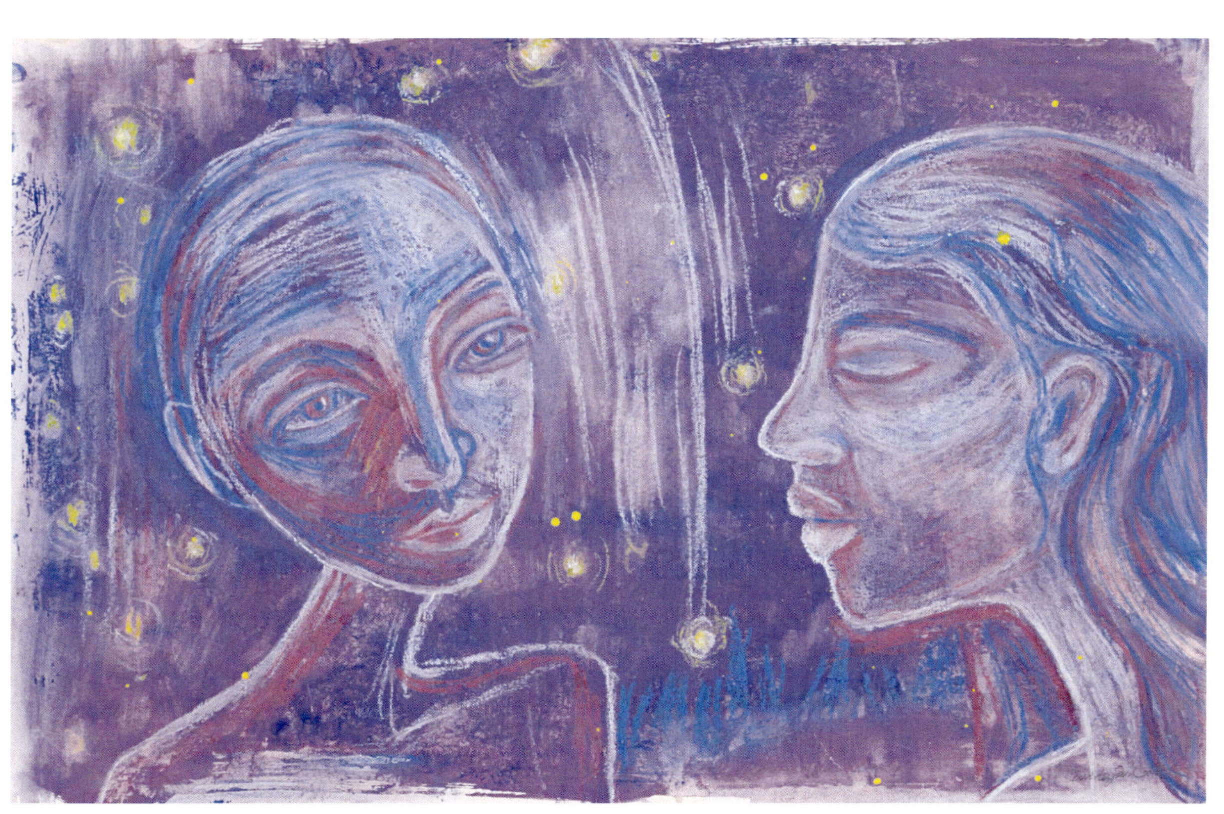

A love that keeps its promises

There are always many stars in the night sky;
stars that remind us of a promise given to Abraham,
a promise to a man great in age without a son,
that he will be the father of many nations,

outnumbering the stars.

A sky that resounds with love and the passing of days.
As the sun rises each morning and the moon shines in the night,
So God is faithful to His promises.

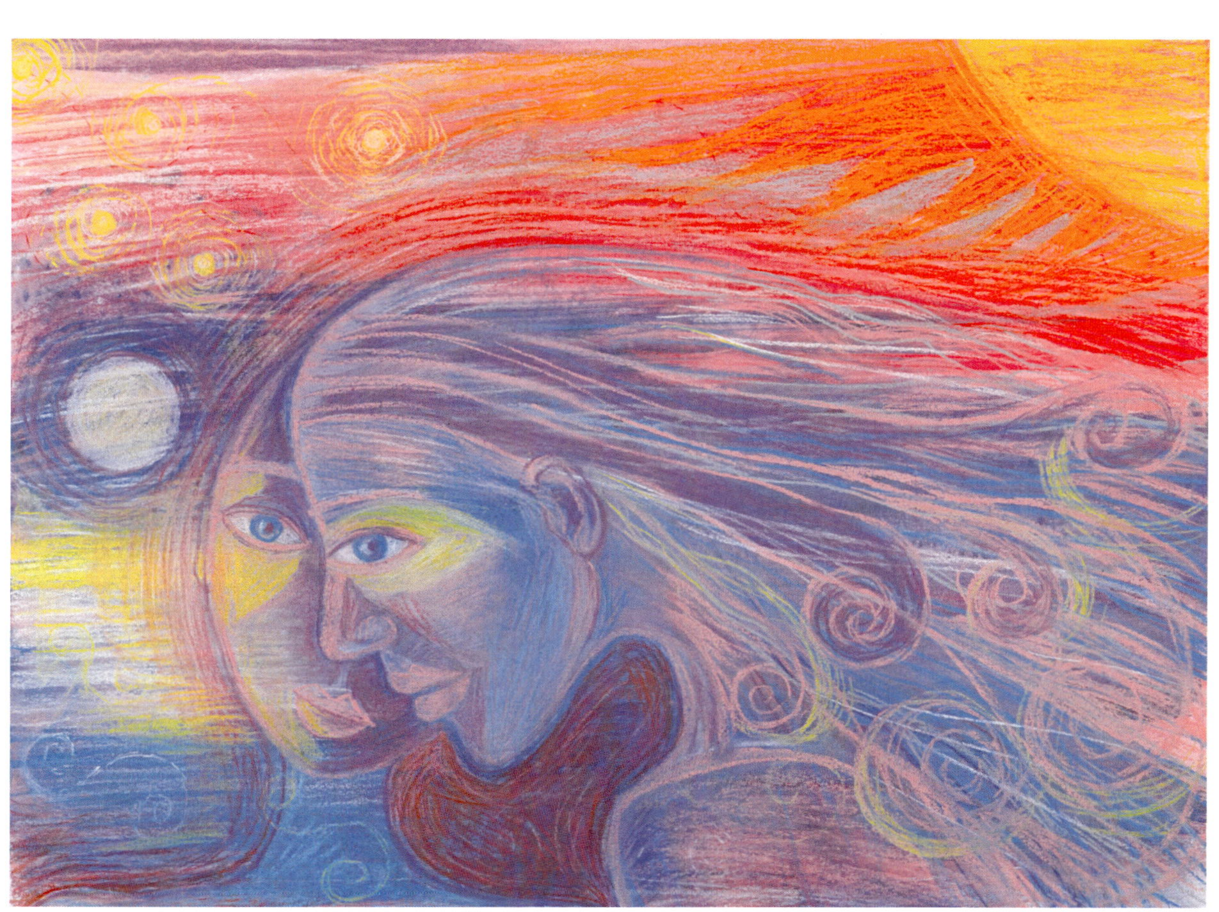

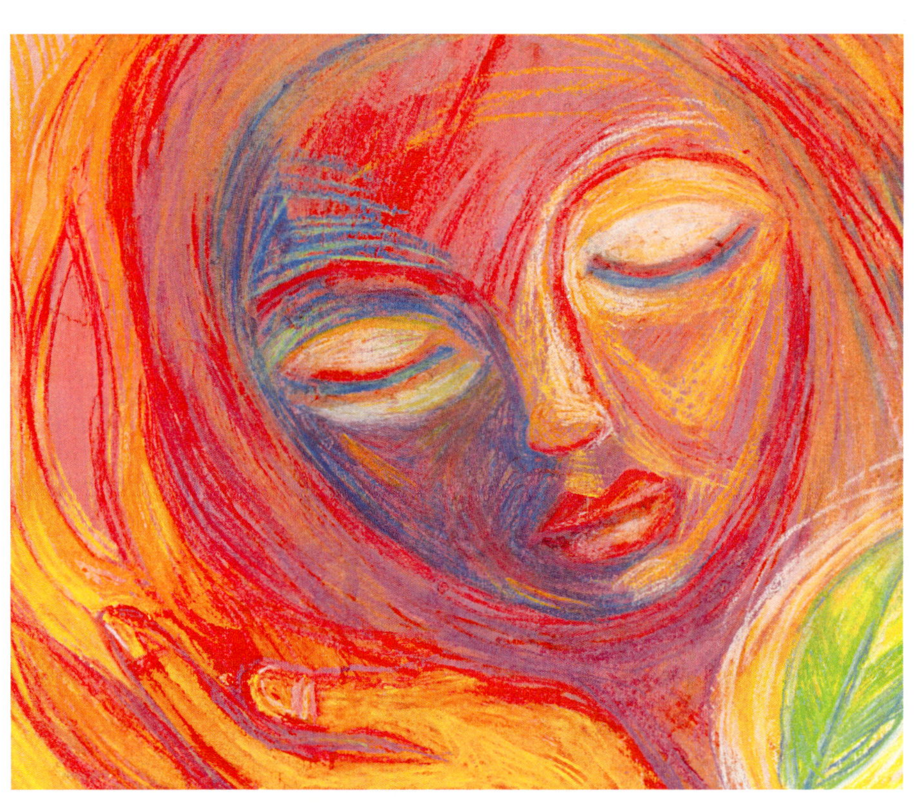

A love that hears your groaning

A prayer is heard.

Prayer is powerful and strong, peaceful and true.

A love that brings you peace

Rest in me – a perfect rest whose mind is stayed on thee.
Close your eyes. Don't focus on your circumstances. Focus on me.
The stars are still shining.

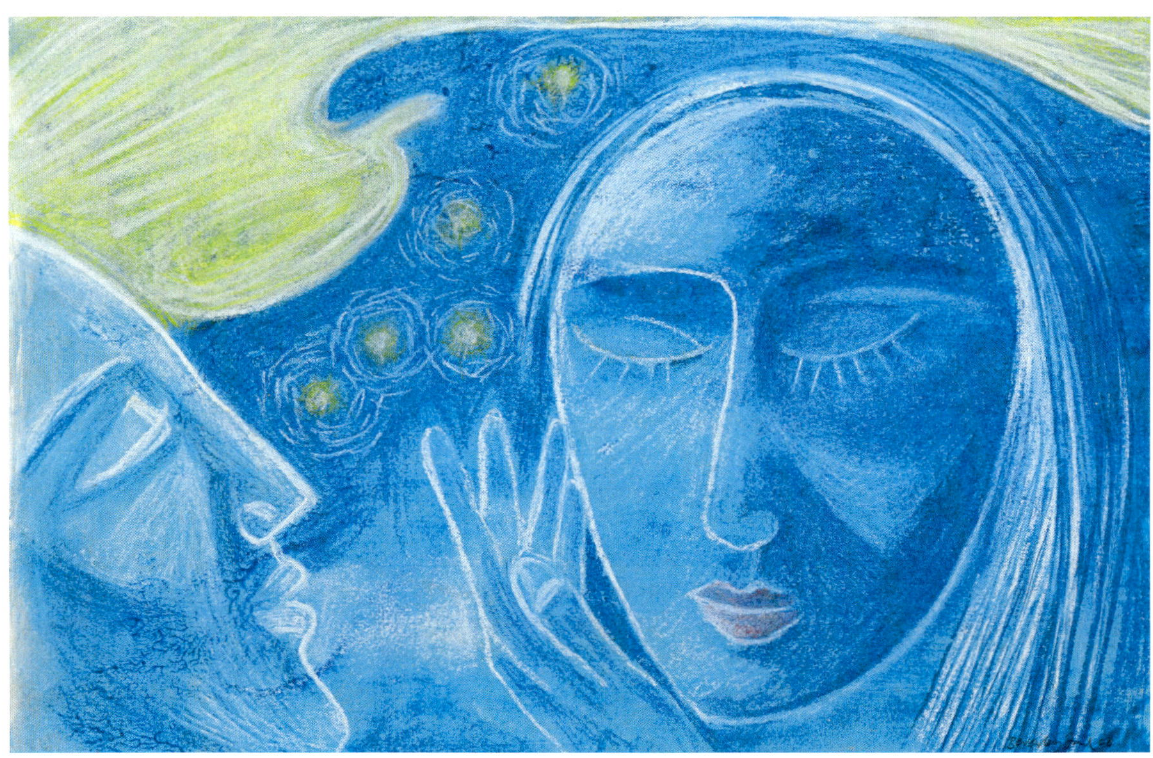

Trust me

Hold on; keep swimming.

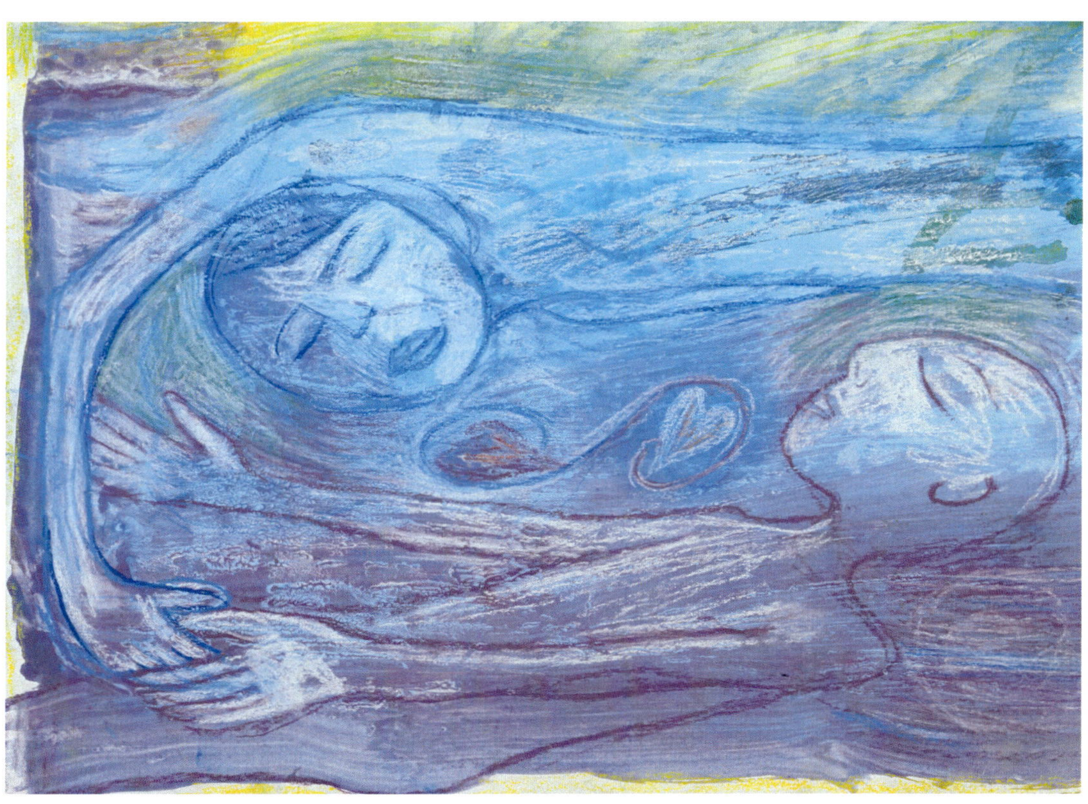

I will lift you up

You will set my feet on higher ground.

A poet once asked if the stranger was waving or drowning.
I was drowning, yet reaching out; if you like, waving –
looking for higher ground.

The more my focus lifts to the stars and the skies;
the nearer my feet rise to the higher ground.

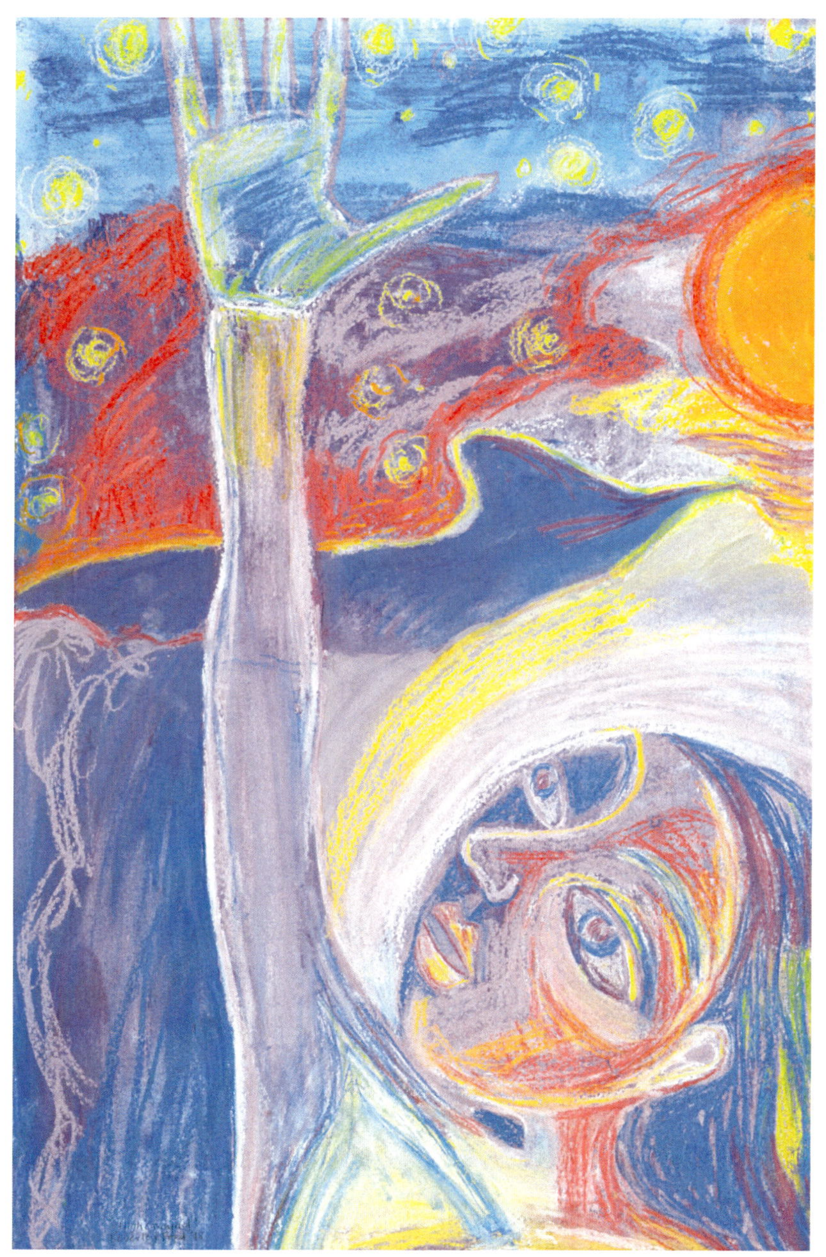

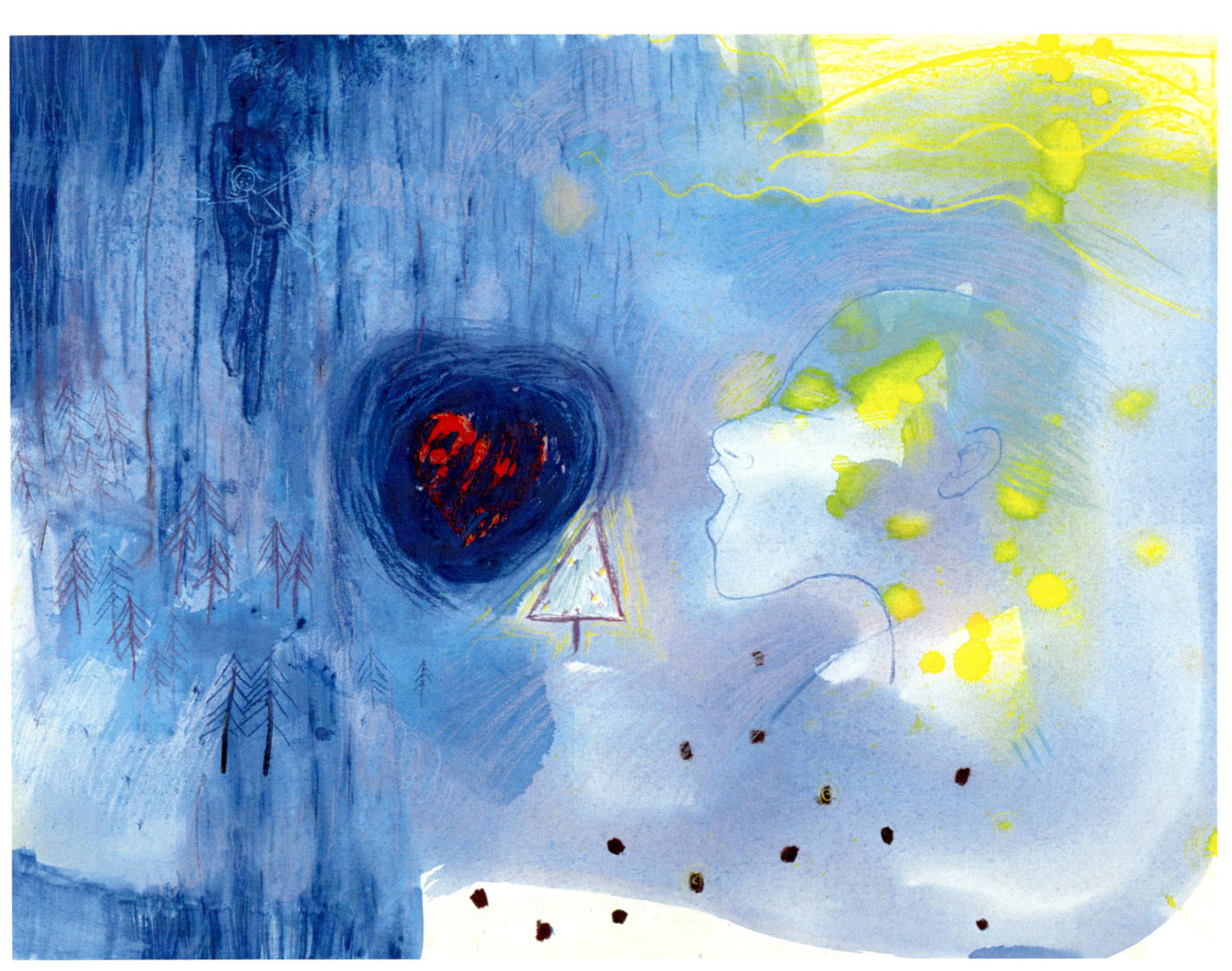

Deep calls unto deep

You will always love me.

Sometimes there is a cry from the heart that reaches way into the depths through a life past and present. The deep heart response is God's cry back from His heart to us.

Release me into the light that I may know your love.

Don’t lose sight

I curl up in a ball.
Your love may be with me but I see no light.
Overwhelmed.
Don’t lose sight.

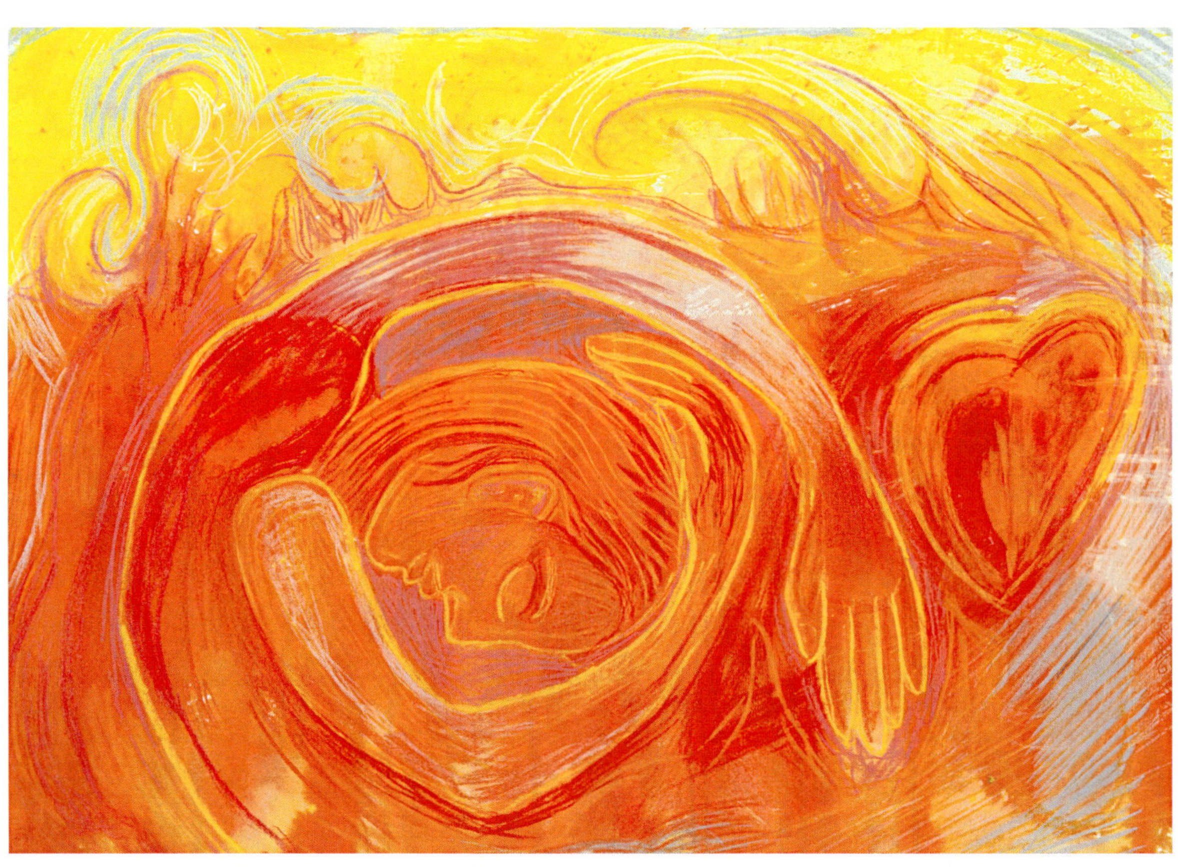

Praise me in the darkness

But I WILL sing your praises. I will unravel myself and lift my hands to you.
I see a mass of confusion all around me, but I will trust that you are in control.

Where things appear to be dark,
I will believe that you can make the sun shine.

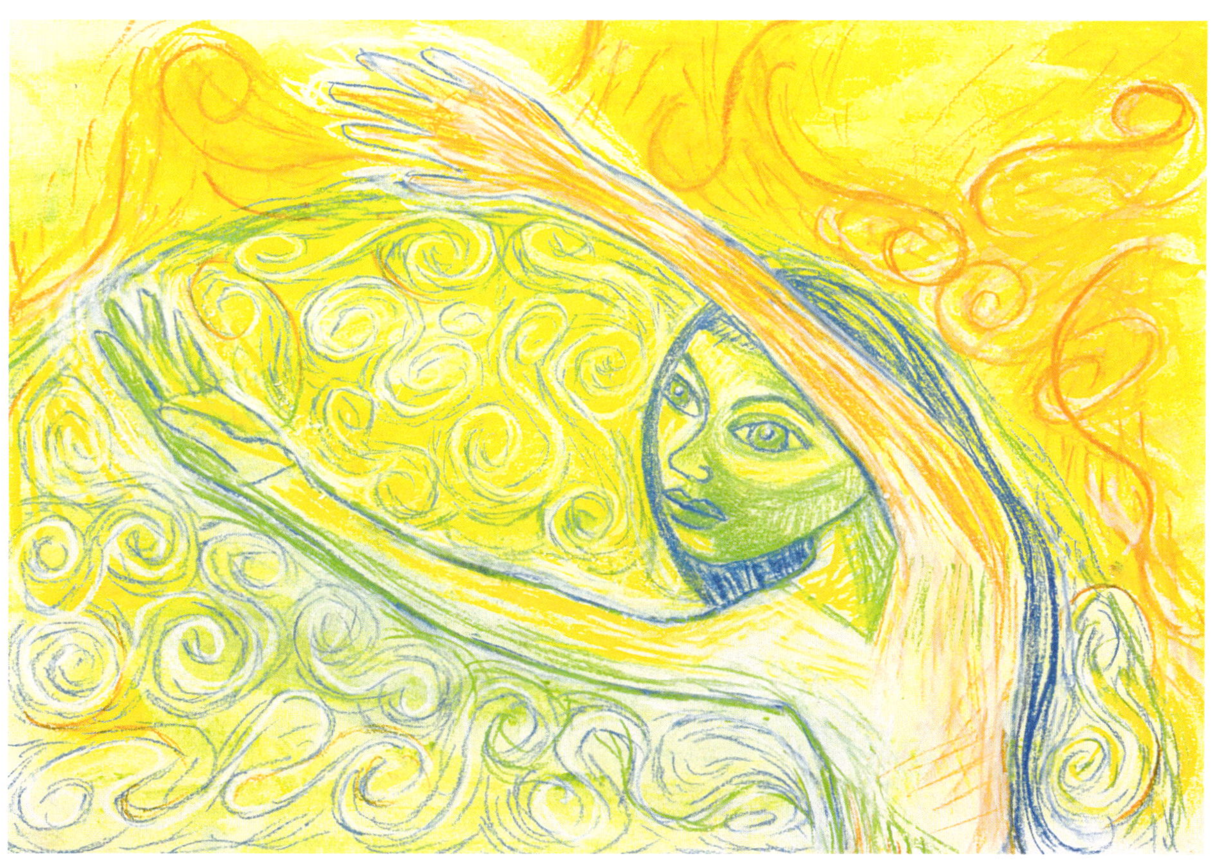

Praise me through the pain

I will love you – you have given me yourself.
A rip and a jewel – pain and resurrection.

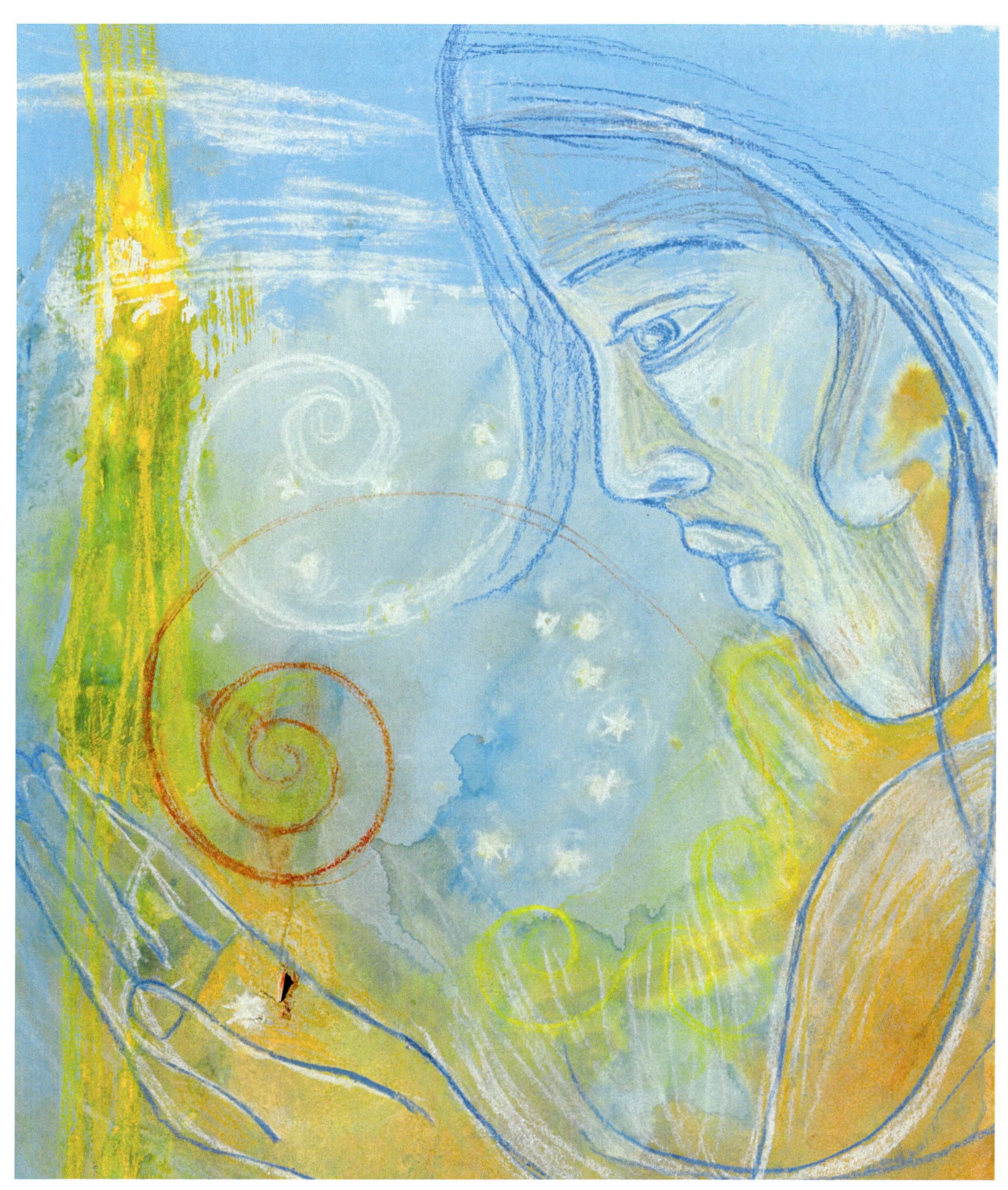

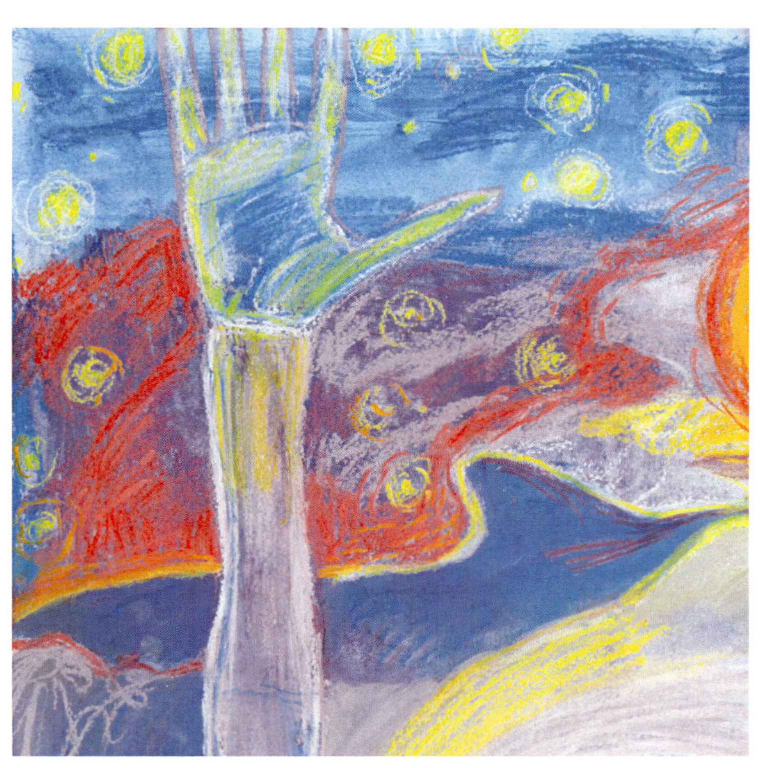

Remember my promises

You remind me of your love for me – Abrahams's stars.

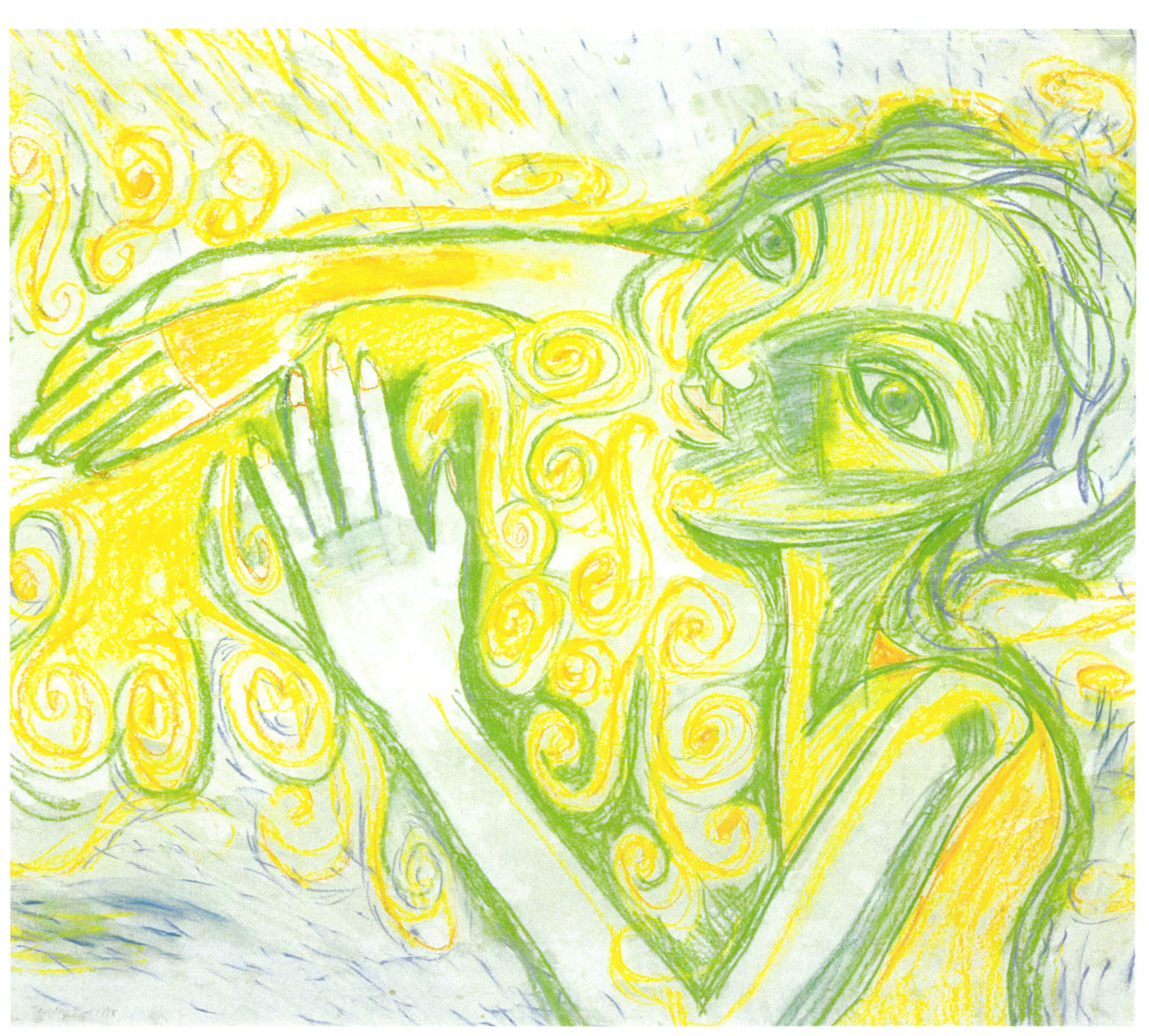

Remember me

I cannot contain you.

Neither are my ways your ways,
Nor your thoughts my thoughts.

A time will come

A promise awaited becomes fulfilled.

One breath, one “Yes” of the Spirit, and the wheels start turning for us
here in time and on this earthly space.

Waiting for you – I’ve learnt to love you in a different way; I’ve learnt that I fail, but you forgive me; I’ve learnt that you’re always there. I’ve learnt that I need you more. I’ve learnt that you love me. I am still learning that you love me.

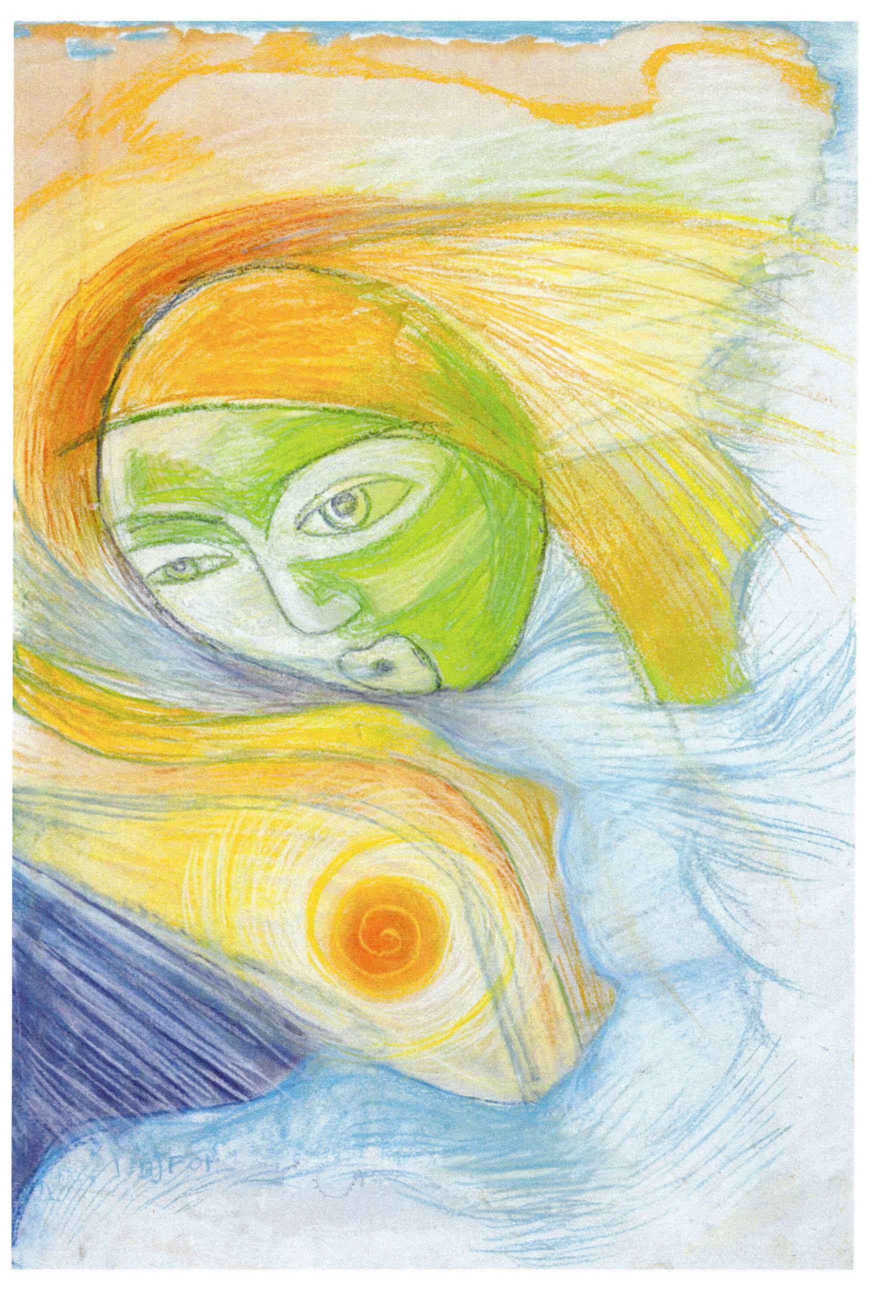

You will hold gold in your hands

I ponder your love for me – you give me gold.

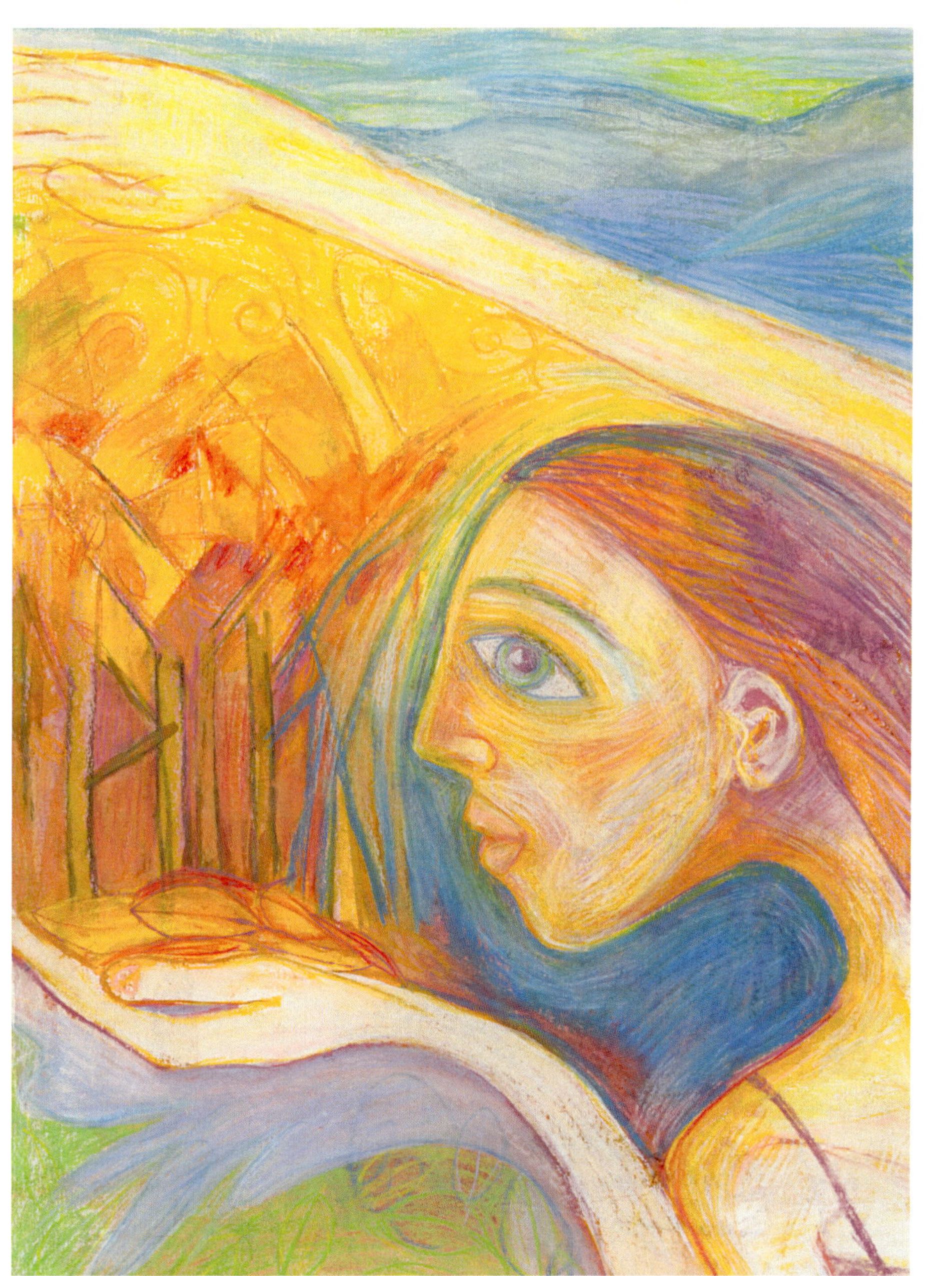

And you will give it away

You have gold ready for the taking.

Dear child, let my love encircle others as it does you.
Realise how my love encircles you.

Look at all these beautiful flowers.
I made them all and your arms cannot contain their number.
Reach out your hands and let me gather them in.

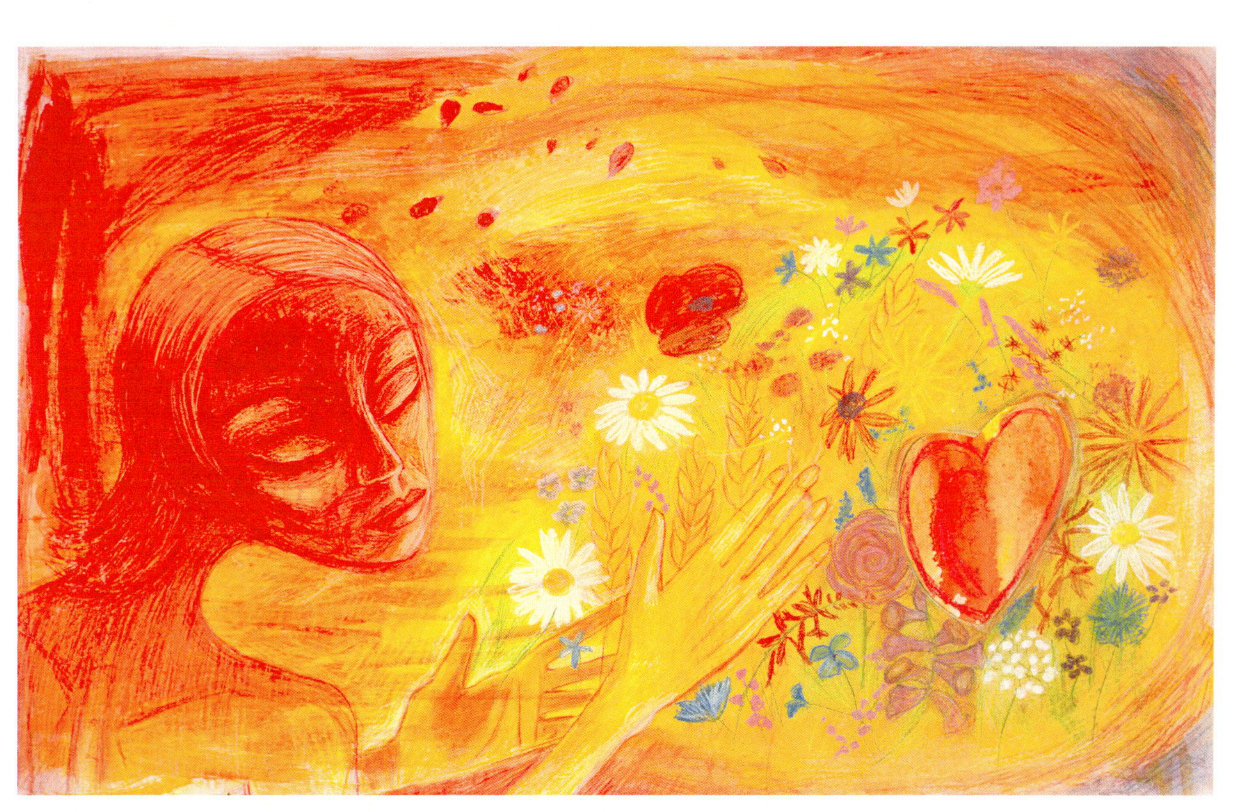

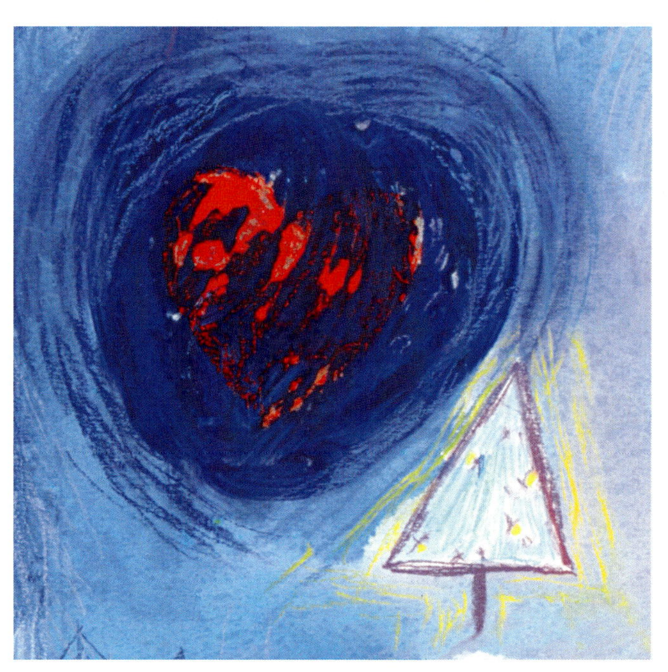

There is hope and there is promise.

There is. I am.

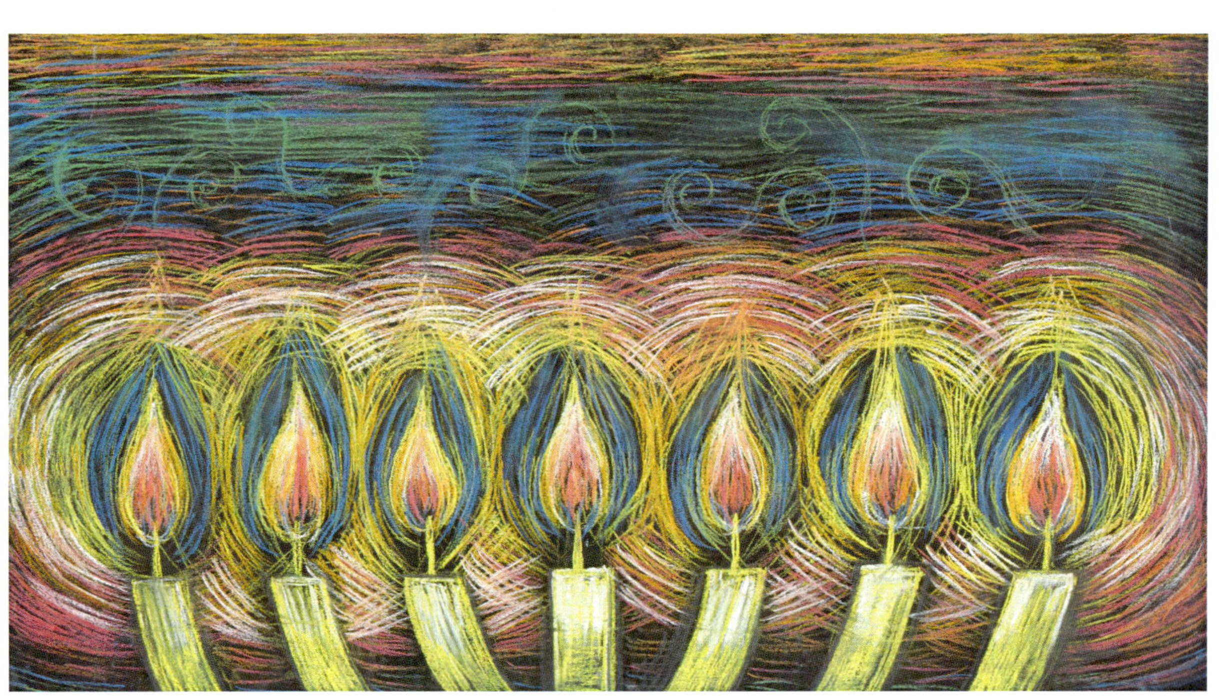

I love you

To God be the glory, great things he has done.

Behold Books

ISBN 978-1-9998372-0-4

9 781999 837204